Raising a Parent

Lessons My Daughter Taught Me
While We Grew Up Together

BY ROCHELLE RILEY

To Martha

Rochelle R.

2010

Credits

Author Rochelle Riley, Columnist, Detroit Free Press

Copy editor Emiliana Sandoval

Project coordinator Steve Dorsey,
Vice President / R+D, Detroit Media Partnership

Book design + cover illustration
Brian McNamara, Principal + Creative Director
Nice Dog Creative Marketing, www.nicedog.us
Book cover concept
Paula Batchelor, www.paulabatchelor.com

Detroit Free Press

615 W. Lafayette Blvd., Detroit, MI 48226, www.freep.com
© 2010 by Detroit Free Press and Church Street Media. All rights reserved. All previously published essays reprinted with permission of the Louisville Courier-Journal and the Detroit Free Press.
Printed by Malloy Inc., Ann Arbor, MI, www.malloy.com

Other books by Rochelle Riley

- "From the Heart: Selected columns by Rochelle Riley" (Louisville Courier-Journal)
- "Life Lessons: Essays on Parenthood, America, 9/11 and Detroit" (Detroit Free Press)

Other Free Press books

- "The Detroit Almanac: 30 Years of Life in the Motor City"
- "Ernie Harwell: Extra Innings with the Voice of Summer"
- Steve Yzerman Hall of Fame Collection
- Eric Sharp's "Fishing Michigan: Tales and Tips from an Avid Angler"

 To order any of these titles, go to **www.freep.com/bookstore** or call **800-245-5082**.

2
Raising
a
Parent

In 1992, I adopted a little girl because I thought she needed me. I soon learned that I needed her, and that, through her eyes, I would see the world in ways I never had before. These essays, written from 1995 through 2007, document the growing-up process for her — and for me.

This book is for her.

Raising a Parent

Special thanks

This book could not have happened without the amazing support of a legion of people that begins with my Aunt Nell, the late Nellie Ruth Lewis, who was with me in the beginning, and my daughter's numerous godmothers and godfathers, both official and unofficial.

It also could not have happened without the friends and colleagues through the years who were five-minute babysitters and ever-ready advisers, tear-wipers and picture-takers. When you're a single parent, it is a special friend who holds the camera when your hands are full. I owe thanks to the former research and archives librarians at The (Louisville, Ky.) Courier-Journal and the Detroit Free Press, especially my friend Shelley Lavey, who aided and abetted nearly every column I wrote.

And finally, I'd like to thank the parents and teachers and librarians from across the state of Michigan who helped students send in drawings for the Detroit Public Library Art Contest to find 13 sketches for this book. Opening the packages felt like Christmas morning. I delighted in the masterpieces, which were delicious, poignant and funny. Each child whose work is featured here is the winner of a $500 scholarship, thanks to the Skillman Foundation, with support from the Lakeshore Engineering Foundation. Each child also gets bragging rights for what may be their first published artwork. You can meet them on page 119.

4

Raising
a
Parent

In the beginning

Nothing prepares you for the arrival.

Not books.

Not people.

Not confidence.

When a living thing comes at you, drooling, pooping, crying and needing, something kicks in from somewhere and you just do.

Whatever it takes.

Every day.

The best you can.

But then, the fun begins. The ride becomes a roller coaster, and total dependence is replaced with a mix of interaction and exploration.

Curiosity didn't kill the cat. It chased the cat down the stairs and out of the house. Curiosity is why the dog is wearing a skirt. Curiosity is why the Cheerios are lined up down the hall and through the house, breadcrumbs to find her way home.

When I adopted my daughter, she was only 2, and I was only kidding myself that I knew what I was doing. But between her five godmothers, two godfathers, my wise Aunt Nell and a few good books, we survived the next three years intact, helped out by angels at day-care and five-minute babysitters in the newsroom. She was a happy-go-lucky kid who, in her eyes, arrived at the door of kindergarten a woman.

Until I let go of her hand.

But then she tentatively let go of mine, and was on her way.

The essays in this book were written from the time my daughter was 5 until she

turned 17, a dozen years.

Just like adults who count our lives in decades — the ought years, twentysomethings, thirtysomethings, fortysomethings, fiftysomething, which we have declared the new middle age — children's first years are categories.

The first category, lasting just a single year, is the one we call "terrible two." I learned that it is a molding year, since most children are who they will become by their 1,000th day.

The next three years, from 3 to 6, are all about discovery. Their little minds and hands discover the world as you discover who they are. This is when they actually try to understand other people instead of just seeing them. They learn that there are other people in the world besides mommy and daddy. They spend hours away from you, hug other people as hard, and you miss them more than they miss you.

6

Raising
a
Parent

The next five, those persnickety years from 7 to 12, mark the years of combat, as they fight to stay little while fighting to grow up.

The final five, 12 to 17, they just fight to grow up. They spend most of their time leaving — for field trips, summer camps, other people's homes — not knowing that we wish for all the world they'd never go.

Over the years, the moments that I've shared with readers about my daughter are the moments that make most readers happy. No politics. (Well, a little.) No arguments about taxes or health care or war and peace. Just the universal knowledge that, no matter who we are or who got our presidential vote, parenthood is a shared ride. It is timeless and frightening; special and overwhelming.

And while we may have thought we were spending years teaching our kids, we come to realize we were learning so much as well.

I know I did.

— R.R.

Raising
a
Parent

5 years old

**Sugar and spice and everything nice ...
and then school begins**

Her first day

I was more scared than she was.

I packed her lunch, helped her dress in her favorite shorts and matching shirt, and let her proceed out of the house in front of me so I could get used to the sight of her walking away.

When we arrived at her new school, she clutched my hand. It was a comforting feeling, knowing that when you're 5, Mom can still make things better.

As we entered her classroom, we tried to decide where "her place" would be. In her open '90s classroom, there are were no rows of desks with A-B-C assignments, just lots of floor space or little tables and the smiling faces of a teacher and aide. Her curiosity got the better of her, and she moved with ease to the "housekeeping center" with its miniature broom, dishes and ironing board, before strolling to the writing center.

She didn't notice right away that I had moved toward the door, to sit by the closet and imagine I was five blocks away, in my office, pretending to work but worried about her.

She began to draw before quickly looking up, terrified at being surrounded only by children. I was afraid she would run to me, lose the comfort she had momentarily gained. But when her gaze caught me sitting by the door, with my legs crossed in a too-small chair, she gave me a small wave with her crayon and continued her art.

I stayed through lunch, and through quiet time, which was called nap time 30 years ago.

And as I watched her pretend to sleep on a mat while playing with her feet, I became 5 again, heading off to an adventure that I could not resist.

There was no fear in a young mind fascinated by books and words and a huge blackboard for endless writing.

10

Raising a Parent

I remember wondering whether I would remember anybody's name, and if I should tell anyone the teacher was my cousin.

That is one remnant of segregated schools I recall fondly. My siblings and I were related to, or close to, nearly everyone there. The principal was my godfather. Some of my friends' moms worked in the cafeteria. We tried nothing, because we knew we could get away with nothing.

I remember trying to remember every detail so I could share them with my mother, for whom teaching had been a joy until illness took her chalk and pointer away.

And as I watched my daughter enjoy her first day of school, I remembered most that nearly every teacher that I ever had was always in the building before I got there and was still there long after I'd left.

And I hoped that my child would realize the importance of the first day of school, hoped that somehow in the monotonous speeches I'd given her about why she had to go to school, she'd mostly hear that school was supposed to be fun.

On the first day of school, you decide what you will be for the rest of the days of your life. A hard worker. A crybaby. A clown. Your life as a student portends your life as a person.

And every first day of every school year gives you new possibilities — and opportunities.

So, today, on her first day of school, as she walks ahead of me, eager to see her classroom, I hope I'll remember other first days and think about first days to come. I plan to watch her walk away, wearing a new dress, carrying her lunchbox. I expect I'll see her walking down halls that don't look much different than those at the W. A. Pattillo School did 30 years ago. I expect I'll see faces that don't look much different

11

Raising
a
Parent

than my Cousin Mary's.

And, if my memory of her first first day isn't clouded by tears and the dust of daily living, I will remember that she had fun. That first first day, as we finished our afternoon activities and packed our things to take home, my daughter looked at me and asked, "Can we come back tomorrow?"

I told her, "Sure, we can come back every day until the weekend."

Her question assured me that she was ready for new sights and sounds, hopes and dreams.

But I also knew she was still my kid when she asked, "But do we still have to come so early?"

Raising
a
Parent

13

Raising
a
Parent

6 years old

**Finding hidden treasure
and surviving road trips**

Finding treasure

Opening drawers is like opening a Dr. Seuss book: Oh, the things that you'll find!

Our wooden havens hold bits of life that we no longer know what to do with, but can't let go.

Hearts, like drawers, are cluttered with memories, good and bad. You like to sort through the good clutter sometimes to remind yourself of pleasant times. You wish you could get rid of the bad things, but they hold on. So you push them aside, intending to throw them away one day.

But you don't.

As I prepare to trade our old home for a new one, I face sorting through memories of life since college. (I never throw anything away.)

There are remnants of great dates and poor decisions, souvenirs from vacations and ill-fated shopping sprees.

There's a rock from a beach in Cancun, Mexico that my daughter decided was the most important item on the continent. There's a pack of Tylenol produced before the '82 scare. (Wonder what that's worth?)

There are chessmen that long ago lost their homeland, place mats that, like siblings, have all moved away from each other and don't resemble anyone in their vicinity now, and a full deck of cards — a miracle!

There are coupons for golf lessons not taken, coupons now expired and phone numbers of people whose names I don't recognize. In one drawer, I find my old manuscripts of The Great African-American Novel.

There are dozens of earrings, all single. (Their mates have escaped and probably

made it to the border by now.) There are hundreds of ticket stubs from my Salvador Dali period; I had planned to do an abstract montage (with oversized clocks) of all the places I had been one year.

There are matches, though I don't smoke, and business cards charting my career across America. There's nail polish from the last formal dance I went to, a to-do list from 1990 and old letters from even older boyfriends.

There are postcards from Cairo and postcards I bought for and addressed to friends, who, evidently, never got them.

These memories stay locked up tight until they are set free to provide a glimpse of past adventures.

Eyeing the junk, or treasure trove, I begin to wonder whether politicians recall things like we do, the rest of us whose only office is life.

Is there a drawer in the Oval Office or the residence kitchen where President Clinton keeps Chelsea's early handwriting? Does he have a copy of the first speech he ever gave or the first letter Hillary wrote to him?

Do politicians savor precious memories the way we do? Do they remember the first time they helped change policy in the same way that a teacher remembers teaching that first child to read?

Or do the nice things get trampled by the should-haves, the no-I-didn't's and the wish-I-hads?

That may be what's wrong with politicians — well, what's wrong with politicians that can be fixed. They need to enjoy the good times more. In striving for that next victory, that next great camera shot, that next speech, they sometimes forget to stop and kiss the baby.

The bundles of should-have-dones need to equal the number of glad-I-dids, so that the clutter they sort through when it's all over will reflect time well spent.

As I separate the really useless items from those that might still have sentimental value, I wonder whether I should call President Clinton to discuss clutter. I can't share state secrets, and he won't discuss foreign policy, but I can share some effective ways to clear clutter.

He could resolve unresolved issues (There's something to be said for finality and moving on.), get rid of the junk that is irrelevant and treat with respect those things that will be with him for a long time. He needs to decide what's needed — universal health care — and what's junk, so he can fight, with conviction, for the important things, and to heck with the rest.

And he'll learn that somewhere in his desk in the Oval Office, along with the assorted papers dictating schedules, policy and a more organized plan for welfare reform, there ought to be a drawing from the first time Chelsea traced her hand.

18

Raising
a
Parent

Road trips

After buying a Nissan minivan (a suburban-mom commando vehicle that inner-city dwellers also use), my daughter and I trek down to North Carolina, where I was born.

It's a 14-hour drive that, for us, requires one overnight stay, 14 bathroom breaks and a couple of "Let's-see-what-that-is!" respites.

At least one stop is a "We're-tired-of-driving-so-let's-stop-at-this-place-because-any-place-with-a-clean-bathroom-must-have-good-Popsicles!" stop. And, sometimes, we just pause to stretch our legs and clean the junk food wrappers out of the car.

As a child, I always said that when I had kids, we would fly everywhere, that these long, cramped car rides were for the birds. Actually, flying is for the birds, and I didn't know why people or animals would schlep across 900 miles of Earth … well, never mind.

But I changed my mind as a driving grownup who learned to appreciate the changing colors of leaves and the comfortable, frosty nip in a fall breeze.

It is important for parents to maintain the tradition of the American vacation, whether in a station wagon or a Winnebago, for children to see through grown-up eyes and glimpse through grown-up wallets what our parents were talking about all those years. It is imperative that at least once, families drive through a few states and do that cost-effective, patriotic, hands-on experiencing of our country.

One recent trip: We're heading east on Interstate 64. She finishes her first pack of Twinkies before the Hurstbourne Parkway exit. At the Gene Synder Freeway, she asks, "Are we there yet?"

We've traveled 17 miles.

She asks every five miles until I suggest we play games. As I entice her to look at the

19

Raising
a
Parent

jutting rocks and majestic greenery between Shelbyville and the Waddy-Peytona exit, she forces me to guess the name of a male character from the movie "Aladdin."

"Genie?"

"No."

"Jafar?"

"No."

"Aladdin?"

"No, Mom. Abu!"

"The monkey?"

"Yes!"

"But you said a man."

"Well, Mom, isn't Abu a man, a boy monkey?"

"Well, actually, he is … "

"How do you know?"

"Let's play another game … '

We celebrate our arrival in each new state with a wild foot-and-hand dance, complete with loud yells and screams. In North Carolina, she makes me read every mileage marker, town sign and restaurant name.

We stay overnight in Raleigh with friends whose two boys greet us as if we were Michael Jackson in the good old days. We eat, reminisce, listen to old music and joke about getting old.

"If you remember Sam Cooke, you're ancient!"

We repack and head the last 70 miles to home. Suddenly, we pass a tiny carnival

20

Raising
a
Parent

clinging to a sliver of grass near a mall. We stop to get flung around in rickety rides and snatch wisps of pink cotton candy from 50-cent cones. We watch little girls make sand art and a baby fret in his stroller, his mouth dribbling juice onto a bright red jumpsuit. Calliope music wafts through the night air, reminding me of long-ago county fairs.

Tuckered, we take off on the last leg of our trip, to the eastern North Carolina house that seemed so huge when I was 6, but seems so tiny now. Much of my hometown has changed, but we drive around to find the sites that haven't. I show my daughter the library where I used to work endlessly, spending off-hours reading brand-new books before putting them on the shelves. We pass the swimming pool where I could swim, and the one where I legally could not, at least for a while.

I drive by the mill where my grandfather worked for nearly 30 years. We keep going, reliving purple-and-gold Viking football games as we pass the town's only high school, sharing blushes as we pass the town commons where I first kissed a boy.

After three days, then tearful goodbyes, we head back to Louisville, and the adventure begins again. And I realize, as we sing at the top of our lungs at the sight of Eastern Kentucky, that vacation isn't always a destination.

Sometimes, it's the getting there.

21

Raising a Parent

Bad words

When I went to screen "Independence Day" to determine its suitability for my 6-year-old, I made a list of things to watch out for: pornography, gratuitous violence, bad words.

Then I wondered whether I would recognize what I was looking for.

Violence that made me shudder 10 years ago now barely causes me to wince. What was considered sexually taboo five years ago now is featured in movies rated PG-13. That leaves only bad words.

I can remember — and I'm not that old — when TV characters couldn't say "damn," no matter what time it was. Now that time of innocence is gone. You cannot shelter your children, or yourself, from bad words. Gangsta rap didn't start it, but it sure has ingrained a sense of looseness and hard talk. As I watch my daughter do the Butterfly, a hip-hop dance where she moves her legs in and out while she bobs up and down, my stomach turns, and I scream.

Six-year-olds should not be allowed such moves.

But it's all the rage, and it fits the music, which is pervasive. You hear it in school, on television and blaring out of those MEUs, mobile entertainment units, better known as teen-driven cars.

At the movies, she and I have a system: If we hear an unmentionable word uttered, we urgently whisper, "Bad word!" to remind us not to take it out of the theater with us.

The system is harder to use now because we have to talk loud enough to drown out the incessant chatter and ringing phones and piercing beepers. But that's another story.

You may say, "Why don't you just boycott the movies with bad words, music that sells sex and TV that lacks character?"

Well, Disney doesn't make enough movies every year. And if you saw the uncharacteristic lust scene in "The Hunchback of Notre Dame," you'd be asking, "What's up with that?!"

We DO pass on a lot of movies and a lot of music. But you can't hide from life. You can try to control every aspect of your child's existence, thinking it's actually possible — until you hear her sing ALL the lyrics of a raunchy Jodeci song and hear yourself asking, "Where did you LEARN that?"

The best we can do is teach our children to distinguish between what they inevitably will hear and what they will hear that they are not to bring home.

When my child is singing Mary J. Blige's song "Not Gon' Cry" from the "Waiting to Exhale" soundtrack (No, I didn't take her to see the movie), and she gets to the line of plaintive regret, "I should have left your a-- a long time ago," she knows she can't say that word. (She's not even allowed to say "butt.") So she mouths it. I can't hear it, but I know it's there.

Still, that means there's hope.

It means she's distinguishing between right and wrong, between can and can't, between being someone you can be proud of and someone who is embarrassing.

I can't kill gangsta rap. Wouldn't want to kill all of it.

But I don't want my child to hear the N-word from anyone, black or white. And I don't want her to lose the ability to recognize right from wrong, good from bad, appropriate from "No, you didn't!"

Not teaching her what's wrong is irresponsible. Not teaching her what's acceptable — or as close as we can get to that day's acceptable — is just as serious. And just as

Raising
a
Parent

irresponsible. Good judgment doesn't grow like fingernails. We must teach it.

Instead of ignoring rap, inappropriate sexual references and bad words, let's teach why what's unacceptable IS unacceptable and when. And let's remember that what's acceptable in one person's house might not be in another's.

Instead of banning discussion, let's have more conversations with our children and with each other about what we are willing to accept in our music, our movies, our lifestyles.

Then maybe our children will become adults who can make wise choices. That means, in my case, I'll keep trying to help my daughter tell the good words from the bad ones.

Even when those words change.

Raising
a
Parent

Raising
a
Parent

7 years old

Learning the economies of life

Teaching economics

It seems like the hardest thing in the world to do: teach kids about money. How to get it, how to spend it, how to save it. But it's even harder when you have to explain how it's taken away.

My friend, Naomi, learned this while making her son and daughter pay for a painting frame they broke while playing ball inside. Naomi decided the pair would pay for the glass by doing extra chores for $4.55 an hour — minimum wage at the time. The kids seemed thrilled to clean and pick up. By week's end, they'd each done about 10 hours worth of work, earning $45.50 each. As they stood hands out to collect, Naomi calculated their pay.

"Before I pay you," she said, "I have to take out for federal taxes."

"OK," they said.

"Then I have to take out for state and school taxes," she said.

Looking more uncertain, their faces fell. By the time she had taken out for their retirement and savings, they had less than $36 — and all of it went to pay for the frame.

"What happened to our money?" her son lamented.

"The same thing that happens to mine," she said.

Her kids now know that money is something to be valued, but not to be taken more seriously than things money can't buy.

Since then, she said, when she gives them their allowance, they pay more attention to how they spend each dollar. Well, her daughter does. Her son spends his whole allowance within an hour of getting it, then has no money for the rest of the week. Her daughter, on the other hand, spends a little, saves the rest. Her daughter will soon be teaching her son how to save.

It was a valuable lesson for her to give her kids; for any parents to teach their children.

One day, they can teach it to those who run our federal government. I still think it's embarrassing for America to be in debt. It's sinful that the federal government occasionally shuts down for budget reasons. The national debt — the amount we owe because of money we've borrowed by selling bonds and other stuff — is up to $3.7 trillion. (With Social Security payments figured in, it rises to $5.2 trillion.)

Some argue that federal spending should be the same as (or less than) federal income. That makes sense in my house. Still, if kids can learn how to better spend money, so can those we elect — whose "allowances" run into the millions instead of into a few nickels. Federal officials and representatives should appreciate "our" money as much as we want our children to appreciate the lessons we give in wise spending.

I used the lesson on my own daughter. She asked for a sandwich, and I created a submarine special that would make Dagwood drool, and proudly set it before her. She took one bite, and as I turned to get her milk, she threw the rest away.

"What did you do that for?" I asked.

"I didn't want any more," she said matter-of-factly.

"Well," I told her. "You owe me $1.81."

She looked horrified.

"Why?" she moaned.

"Because that's how much those things in that sandwich cost — the bread, the meat, the cheese."

"But I don't have any money!" she told me.

"That's OK. We'll figure something out."

29

Raising
a
Parent

That night at the supermarket, she craved a chocolate bar.

"Can I have this?"

"How much is it?" I asked her.

"Only 55 cents."

"No, you may not have it. But you only owe me $1.26 now."

She pouted and put it down. By the end of two days of "No's," her pout was nearly dragging the ground. But she got over her anger and eventually learned how almost everything cost something.

On a subsequent market excursion, she asked for a bag of chips.

"Sure," I said.

"What's the catch?" she asked.

"No catch. You don't owe me anymore."

"Well, give me a dollar," she said.

"Why?" I asked.

"So I can pay for it myself."

She did, and then she gave me the change. Then she said: "I owe you 72 cents."

She'd learned.

Birthdays

As the years pass, and we celebrate the glories and survive the screw-ups of daily life, it's easy to understand why we forget that every day is a human highlight film.

It's not limited to sports. We all have moments of pure bliss that we need to call up more often, to relive and to encourage others to believe they'll experience, too. A great time to rerun those moments is on birthdays. Birthdays are bookmarks that hold our place in life. They offer us an annual chance to reflect on what was really important in the past and what to pay attention to in the future. They give us a chance to stop and breathe and figure out which race we're supposed to be running: cross-country, marathon or sprint. If we're not sprinters, we need to slow down. If we're not into endurance, we need to pace ourselves.

But birthdays also are supposed to be fun; always have been. Every time I attend one of the many parties on the calendar I keep for my daughter, whose social life has surpassed mine in complexity and depth for a number of years, I have as much fun as the girls. Whether they're skating, swimming, riding in bumper cars or just smashing cake into their faces, those giggles define what celebrating should be.

Birthdays in the old days, as some of my new fourth- and fifth-grade friends call my youth, were more subdued. "Ice cream and cake" was a big deal. If you had hats, you were really doing something! And those memories are supposed to last a lifetime.

As I celebrate another birthday, I realize that I'm still thrilled, in my 30s, when I get my annual birthday card from my grandmother with a dollar tucked inside. Birthdays teach us patience. And that patience is what we use to learn new things. For example, teaching my daughter the elements of time takes much time. But since birthdays taught me to make things fun, I try to use fun to make a point.

Raising
a
Parent

"How long does it take to get to school each morning?" she asks.

"It takes as long as an episode of 'I Love Lucy,' " I tell her. (Thank goodness for Nickelodeon!) Rushing along the interstate to Rupp Arena to watch her favorite Wildcats play, she eagerly asks again and again: "How long will it take to get there?" As long as "Aladdin," I tell her.

A runny nose and fever sends us rushing to the doctor, and she wonders: "Is this going to take long?'

"Two 'Lucy's' and a 'Rugrats'," I tell her. Birthdays also remind you that taking stock is a requirement, not a pleasure. It is the only guaranteed time all year that you will stop for a minute to think. You can never foresee all the changes that will take place in your life, especially when you become responsible for someone else — a child, a husband, a friend. You never knew that set of fake food and huge tea set you bought for Christmas would become a seven-course meal on a Friday night when all you want to do is crash. You learn that it makes all the difference in the world to a child if you decline a reservation for such a fine meal. Many children grow up believing that no one has time for them, except on birthdays.

But for children, every day should be a birthday, another day to learn about life and what things mean. It's too soon for them to reflect, because they're still building memories.

They must benefit from this patience we're learning with each birthday. So the next time a child invites you to a drag race he's hosting in the living room, or to her restaurant for plastic hot dogs and a 1996 bottle of H2O over ice in neat little wine glasses, just drag yourself over there and have a seat. Enjoy the meal, all seven courses of it.

Pretend it's your birthday.

Raising
a
Parent

8 years old

**Being single parents,
learning quiet lessons and
dispensing discipline**

Kids need "the look"

It has taken six years, but I have finally mastered the look.

You know the one.

It's the same one my grandmother gave us in the second pew of our small church in North Carolina when we were fidgeting, giggling, talking or playing — that withering, peripheral stare that took two seconds, but lasted two hours.

One sting from that look and you didn't move.

It was the same look she used in the grocery store if we grabbed something from the shelf without asking. It took less than a second for us to put whatever it was back.

I can do it now. And my daughter hates it.

"Mommie, don't look at me like that."

That look can only be earned, honey, I tell her. That look has kept me out of a lot of harrowing situations, some I didn't foresee.

You're never too old for that look, although its withering qualities fade when you've reached your 30s and have children of your own. That look can keep you from getting burned, diffuse tense situations or stop a train toward harsher discipline before it's left the tracks.

There was a time when parents spanked their children, and those children wouldn't dream of debating something as simple as keeping a room clean or running in the street or doing homework. In those times, parents raised not only their own children, but their friends' children. I remember how Miss Anna B., who used to run the little store on the corner of our street, would give us that look if we weren't polite. Then she'd fuss at us. Then she'd call our grandparents to let them know.

Raising
a
Parent

That look has built the character of many children for generations. It saved me from harm and tragedy.

These times need more parents willing to use "the look." Some of our kids need it. And when I say our kids, I mean all of them, not just the ones who live in our homes.

We see young people doing things that are wrong, and we avert our eyes, look the other way. Saying something is out of the question, because some of these kids have anger so strong they'd just as soon shoot you as look at you.

On the drive to my daughter's school for lunch one day, I saw three boys, about 14, walking across the street, slowly, very slowly, against traffic. I had to actually stop the car for them to pass, they took so long.

I looked at them. I didn't avert my eyes.

They looked back and saw me looking.

I didn't roll down the window and say, "Why aren't you in school?" like Robbie Valentine, the former University of Louisville basketball player-turned-youth counselor, would have. But I'm not 6 foot 6 and more than 200 pounds. But I didn't speed up, like I would have done a week before.

And I didn't look away. I wanted them to know I was looking, and seeing, and caring that they were not where they were supposed to be.

I hoped that in that few seconds, they got a sense of what it feels when someone pays attention to you instead of ignoring you; wonders about you instead of just wishing you weren't there.

For several blocks, I kept kicking myself. Why didn't I stop? Why didn't I find out why they weren't in school?

37

Raising a Parent

Fear.

The fear of young people in this community and others has gotten so strong that it rules us. It followed me from that intersection in West Louisville all the way to school. It followed me back to work, and it's sitting here beside me. It's not a comfortable feeling. So I plan to keep working on the look. I won't avert my eyes. You can't see a problem with your eyes closed. And kids can't see concern if we won't face them.

Maybe the next time, I'll stop and say good morning. I'll ask a question, or show that I care. The kids in trouble need the attention, someone to challenge them, to make them see that we haven't totally given up.

Or have we?

38

Raising a Parent

Single parents

My favorite new commercial features an executive getting her three girls ready to spend the day with a babysitter while she works.

She races around as the girls pack lunches, eat breakfast and moan about not going to the beach.

She tells her daughters she can't romp in the sand because she has an important meeting with a client.

And there's the moment: One daughter looks at her with doleful eyes and says, "Mom, when can I be a client?"

Mom eyes the phone, eyes her responsibility, looks her guilt straight in the eye and says, "You have five minutes to get ready to go to the beach or I'm going without you."

The strains of my favorite Cyndi Lauper song, "Girls Just Want To Have Fun," rise above squeals and laughter.

The next scene shows Mom running along a beach, three girls in tow. She gets comfortable in the sand while the girls play ball.

Then the phone rings, and once again the phone company brings your work to you.

This isn't a lament about phone interruptions or guilt. This is about a trend, one I first noticed during my favorite movie of all time (this week), "Toy Story."

For his birthday, a little boy named Andy gets a brand-new action figure that replaces an old cowboy as his favorite toy. His mom bought the action figure. She plays host at his birthday party. She takes him to Pizza Planet. She moves the family to a new house.

Suddenly, I realized I'd seen this sign in other Disney movies: Single Parent At Work. Single parenting has been a subtle, underlying theme in several Disney movies.

39

Raising
a
Parent

And many Disney children, like my daughter, are being raised by one parent. Cinderella survived a single parent: her awful stepmother. Belle left her single father, Maurice, to live with the Beast.

The Little Mermaid challenged the nerves of her single father, King Triton. And Pocahontas lived for her father, Chief Powhatan, until she met John Smith. Aladdin was an orphan in love with a princess being raised by her father, the sultan, alone. And Pinocchio was adored by a single parent, his loving maker, Geppetto.

All of these great characters were products of single-parent households. Granted, some of the parents weren't the best. But each child triumphed, showing that even under less-than-ideal circumstances it is possible to live happily ever after.

It is a noble effort, showing families that all families are not the same. Judging from the age of these movies, having a single parent — much as we overblame it for children's problems — is neither new nor life-threatening. The number of single-parent households is rising every year. One in four is headed by a single parent, according to a 1995 census survey, the latest available. That's up from one in five in 1980.

Divorce has been as responsible for the trend as births without marriage. The proportion of children living with one parent because of divorce, 38 percent, was only three points higher than children living with a never-married parent. It isn't easy.

As a single parent, I can't toss the ball or the duties to a fellow running back. Girl Scout meeting? I'm there. Soccer practice? I'm there. Violin lessons? There.

Single parents actually are double parents, two parents in one. They do twice the work and handle twice the crises of parents with partners. There is no "Wait 'til your father gets home" or "Your mother's going to be very disappointed." With us singles, the kid

gets one view, representing both parents, at once. Even when you're raising a child alone — by choice and with financial means — it's a daunting responsibility. But imagine the hardships of the surprise single parents who aren't prepared emotionally or economically.

Here's a salute to those who do it well and to those who try. When things go well, take a well-earned vacation. When they don't, take a well-deserved break. The responsibilities will be there when you get back. And if you screw up, and it's not too bad, don't worry.

You get another chance tomorrow.

41

Raising
a
Parent

Quiet lessons are tonic for the soul

He was quiet, soft-spoken, and seemingly undeterred by anything. I was a frantic, impatient mom who had just left the doctor with an 8-year-old who'd used her arm as sandpaper while stumbling into first base during a mean game of kickball.

The pharmacist stood, efficient in white jacket and glasses, in front of shelves containing zillions of drugs. We were headed home to do arm repairs and watch the season premiere of "Mad About You" to learn what Paul and Jamie named the baby. It was 15 minutes before 8.

Suddenly, he said something about a problem with my insurance card, the one that lets you pay $12 for a $10,000 prescription. OK, I told him, wallet in hand. Forget the insurance. I'll just pay for it. Ever patient, he tried to make the card work again. And I was losing my temper. Two hours at the doctor's office and homework to be done made me eager to get home.

"I've never had a problem with my card before. I'd really rather not wait." He never blinked. He didn't get perturbed. He never shared my anxiety. And he never lost patience, even though I know he could hear me tapping my foot at that point. Twenty minutes later he came to the counter, prescription in hand, and politely explained how to use the skin cream and antibiotics. Would I please sign the form saying I'd listened and had no questions? "Sorry it took so long," he said, with a smile, "and if I find out what the problem is at the insurance company, I'll call you, OK?"

"OK."

I hurried out, vowing never to return. But the next day, I got a call. He really had checked and found the problem. Seems my insurance company doesn't handle

prescriptions anymore. My employer hired an entirely different company for that. When I got my new card, he said, he'd gladly give me a refund.

A friend in our human resources office said that sure enough, I was among "a bunch of people" who had mistaken our new cards for junk mail. The next day, I drove to the drug store to apologize and get still another prescription. I dreaded going in because of my previous behavior. I remember thinking that the pharmacist, the quiet man who never lost his temper, had every right to be rude, if he wanted.

I approached the counter, speech ready.

But …

I had to wait.

And you know what I found: the lesson I'd missed the first time. The first time, I was too impatient to look at stuffed animals with my daughter, or poke through magazines, or compare the latest antihistamines.

This time, I stopped to take a look around and discovered the drugstore from my youth — tall, overcrowded shelves of bandages, creams, tonics and enemas, books and sunglasses, Princess Diana bios and a blood-pressure machine. (That's a recent addition.)

It was a place to find everything except pots and pans. There were magazines and Halloween costumes and a smell that reminded me of licorice mixed with Mr. Clean.

My daughter and I compared scary masks, read Winnie-the-Pooh books and studied the new candies on display. I picked up cigars for my grandfather and lipstick that looked better on Tyra Banks. When our prescription was ready, we were reluctant to leave the lions and bears and plastic high heels with matching fake jewelry.

We'd had fun.

I stepped up to the counter, no longer sheepish, and said I was sorry. But it wasn't really necessary. Jake Wishnia, the eternally cool pharmacist, just smiled and wished us good evening. That's the thing about truly nice people. They don't have to remember to be nice. They teach you lessons without anyone knowing you've been in class, except you and God. They teach you to slow down.

Now my daughter and I have a new place to hang out — at least every time she takes a bad slide into first base.

Thank you, Mr. Wishnia.

Prepare kids for once-fictional terrors

I will never forget my brother forever ruining weekly TV dramas for me.

My grandmother and I were watching "The Wild, Wild West," hands clenched, eyes transfixed on our 21-inch, black-and-white screen, waiting to see whether Jim West and his sidekick, Artemus Gordon, would escape a horrendous death at the hands of Dr. Michaelito Loveless. Suddenly, my brother walked past, sandwich in hand, and said, "You know they're gonna make it. They have to be back on next week."

And there you have it.

His words stole the drama and tension from that moment and brought us back to reality. Sure enough, West escaped, and so did Loveless — meaning they would meet again in about six weeks.

It didn't end with "The Wild, Wild West." My brother's words lingered, stealing the drama and tension from every weekly series I've seen since. It's hard to believe any main character is ever really in danger.

The Robinsons remained "Lost in Space." Baretta and that daggone bird survived life-threatening mishaps. And Spenser could be hired again in seven days. It was just awful.

But a few weeks ago, I saw a bigger lesson. My daughter and I were watching an episode of "Early Edition." Among our favorite programs, it is the kind of PG-drama that my 8-year-old can understand and learn from.

The hero was in trouble, and my daughter was worried.

"He'll be OK," I told her.

"How do you know?" she asked.

"Because he has to be back on next week," I said.

45

Raising
a
Parent

She studied on that for a minute, soothed. Then the heavens opened to reveal all.

"So what is the guy's name?" she asked me.

"Gary Hobson."

"No, what is his real name?"

"Kyle Chandler. An actor."

"And he doesn't really get the paper with tomorrow's news in it, does he?"

"No."

"And that's not real blood on 'ER,' is it?" she asked, referring to a program I won't let her watch.

"No."

"O-o-o-o-h-h-h-h."

Now she understands.

The TV world is one where people can, like cartoons, be shot, beaten, attacked viciously, but bounce back, Wile E. Coyote-like each week. In the real world, however, we used to live in Mayberry, content more often than not. The top of the 6 o'clock news wasn't always a homicide.

But somewhere in the years since my brother pushed reality into our television, it seems that the TV world became our real lives. That's right; they switched places.

All the shoot-'em-up series, murder mysteries and gory horrors that once existed only on the screen are now our everyday existence, and the mundane, safe lives we used to fight for have set up shop on television.

I mean, think about it: At one time in life, twisted killers existed mostly in nightmares and bad television, right? And it's no coincidence that current TV audiences are flocking

to shows with happy endings, angels and good guys. (Or shows with no basis in reality that we can prove. Something is out there, but neither we nor Agent Mulder may ever know what.)

Dramatic television — even the Nickelodeon brand — has helped me prepare my daughter for the newscasts she can't escape and the deaths of people she may know. It makes her less horrified by events. I'm not sure whether that is good or bad. But it's better than being overwhelmed.

I want her to be shocked by drive-by shootings, kidnappings, missing kids. No, I'd really rather she be ignorant of them. But that would be irresponsible. It's better to learn and discuss fictional horror so that she's prepared when it confronts her in real life. And we cannot control those confrontations, no matter how much we shelter our kids. Life has become television — movie-of-the-week, terror-filled, deadly.

Man, I wish some of these kids could have seen "The Wild, Wild West." Back then, we didn't think about whether the heroes would escape and return the next week. They just did. We need our heroes to be back next week. We need to make our children believe they will be.

47

Raising
a
Parent

9 years old

**Bad words, embarrassing moms
and "When did your feet get so big?"**

A sole-searching rite of passage

It was bound to happen. It is as sure a rite of passage as eighth-grade graduations, proms and first bras. You know it will come, and it will surprise you in its painfulness, because it reminds that the years are passing more quickly than you'd like. It is at least as painful as when they no longer let you kiss them goodbye in front of their friends, or no longer let you button their shirts.

During a shopping trip to pick up back-to-school shoes, my daughter and I headed for the children's area. She wore a size 4 the week before, so I thought I was ahead of the game. After careful consideration, we found a neat pair of sneakers to try. And try she did, mightily, to get into that shoe. But her foot would not go in.

"It's too small," she finally declared.

"My, your foot has grown again!" I said with more matter-of-factness than I felt. A pleasant saleswoman with children of her own came over. "Can I help?" she asked.

I looked at her with a total sense of helplessness in my eyes. I wanted to tell her no, she couldn't help — not if she couldn't slow down the passing years, not if she couldn't keep my daughter at this place where nightmares still cause tiny feet to pad into my room and ask, "Can I sleep with you?"

Not unless she could help her still get supreme joy from licking a bowl of icing, playing with Legos, watching "Rugrats" or talking with Mr. Bimbo, who lives in her thumb. But I couldn't tell her no. She had to help me find shoes. I asked for the larger children's sizes. The good news, the saleswoman told me, was that shoes existed for my child. The bad news was that they weren't in the children's section.

"She's now into adult sizes," she said with a smile. I had to sit down. My daughter, we

50

Raising
a
Parent

soon discovered, my 9-year-old future model-nurse-reporter-president, wears a ladies' size 5 and a half.

The saleswoman didn't even laugh at me when I asked whether any of them came with Velcro. She understood.

"My 9-year-old wears a 7 ladies' shoe," she said.

We searched and searched to find the least sophisticated, non-sexiest, flattest shoes. We found cute sandals and tennis shoes, more like mine than my daughter's college-basketball knockoffs with Barbie or Skydancers on the side.

My daughter oohed and aaahed as she tried on shoes like Mommie's, while Mommie sat staring at the size 4's, thinking of cutting off the toes, like the old women in my neighborhood did when shoes got too small:

"Those are my favorite shoes. I can still get some wear out of them."

As we left, I watched my daughter bounce up and down, curls going back and forth as she turned to point things out to me. She used to be only as high as my knees. Now when she stands in front of me, the top of her head nearly touches my chin. Other signs of growth abound. She laughs when I suggest silly little games we used to play. She kicks my butt at Mancala, wants to help me balance my checkbook (I got her her own.) and really wants to watch "Living Single" with me on Thursday nights. She also is constantly tossing out shirts, shorts and dresses that are too small.

"Can't wear this one anymore!" she proclaims as she tosses one into the Salvation Army basket. She is oblivious to my pain and my efforts to keep her little. She can't wait to grow up. I remember when I was like that, and my grandmother would tell me, "If you could only know what I know now."

Raising
a
Parent

I've even said it to my daughter: "Honey, when I was your age, I was ready to be a big girl. Now I wish I could be a little girl again."

Her only response is, "You were my age once?"

There will be more rites of passage, more days when she does something I once did. I never understood the big deal when those things happened to me, causing my grandmother to get teary-eyed and proclaim, "You're growing up."

Now I do.

Raising
a
Parent

When least expected, daughters mimic moms

Raising a child is like having heaven. It's all you want, but you're never ready.

You wish for it, work to get it, but don't really know what you're in for. No one can really tell you all the things you will face, all the things that are so unpredictable, yet happen to all children.

As parents, we're never really sure how we're doing until life provides glimpses into the future.

Mothers have special relationships with daughters because we are the women they sometimes become.

We are their ultimate role models, even if they admire Madonna or Janet Jackson or their teachers. The person they emulate most when it's time to put on tights, or adjust a slip strap or put on lipstick — even if only in the house — is mom. We are usually the ones they ask about boys. And we are the ones in whom they see maternal reflections that won't be clear for years to come. Being a good mom can run in the family.

My daughter is showing me that I must be doing a few things right. Oh, she has teased a playmate or two or stretched my patience like a rubber band. I've seen her yell at a kid hard enough to hurt his feelings, working her neck in that way that I can't quite get. But I've also watched her give her entire lunch to a friend who was hungry or give her coat to a classmate who was cold.

I saw her lose a good friend and gain her back all within one week.

She has shown me examples of what parents look for each day, some sign that what you're trying to teach is catching on and showing through. She recently gave me another example.

53

Raising
a
Parent

I had been felled by some awful illness that was either the world's worst sinus infection or that new strain of flu that arrived from Australia by way of Bardstown Road and was attacking the populace like kamikaze pilots.

For at least two days, my goal in life was to get up and walk to the kitchen without pain. My head was as sensitive to air as it was to the ringing telephone. It was then that my daughter showed me that she truly is a caring, loving human being.

The doctor had prescribed medicine designed by someone who believed sleeping it off is as effective as actually killing any virus. All that day I was a druggy, sleepy, loony mom.

That night we worked on homework on my bed. Then my daughter went off to play while I read a little while watching CNN. I didn't remember falling asleep. But I did remember waking up during the night without my glasses. The television and lights were turned off.

I remember checking on my daughter and finding her sound asleep, one of her "people" from her collection of stuffed animals and dolls snuggled beside her.

The next morning I mentioned what had happened. My daughter giggled and told me what I already knew, that she had crept into my room, slipped my glasses gently from my face, turned off the TV and lights and tiptoed off to bed.

At first, I was stunned.

It seemed impossible that my daughter could move around and do things at night without my knowing. After all, I had heard every sound, every footstep, every whimper, every cry from a nightmare — for years! Even now, in a crowded classroom, across a playground, along the vast corridors of malls, I, like most parents, can hear my child from 40 yards away and pick out her voice.

I've put her to bed thousands of times, only to hear a whispered, "Mommie, come back" within minutes. And that whisper would bring me back.

Sometimes at night, she tests me. She sneaks out of bed to see whether I can hear her. And I always call out, "Where are you going?" — a question that elicits squeals and a rush back to bed.

The idea that she had put me to bed, tucked me in, was as strange as it was moving and delightful. I learned two lessons: I must be doing something right, and she'll make a great mother one day.

Raising
a
Parent

Mom's job is to embarrass

It has become apparent to me now. Every day, in some way, for the rest of my life, I will embarrass my daughter by doing "momly" things. It happens so often now that I have girded myself for steely looks and plaintive cries of "Oh, M-o-o-m-m!"

I'll give you an example. As a young girl being raised by a grandmother who had already raised two daughters and really knew what she was doing, I told myself a dozen times, no, at least two dozen times, that when I became a mom, I would never, ever lick my fingers and use them to wipe my child's face.

What could be worse?

But the memories must have faded, because it happened on the way into Highland Presbyterian Church for her violin recital. She had a little something, a bit of doughnut, speck of milk, who knows, on her cheek. And I didn't think twice before licking my index and middle fingers and applying them to her face. "Yuck!!!" she screamed as she brushed my hand away. "Don't put spit on me!"

For a moment, I heard myself, saying the same thing to my grandmother, only not quite so forcefully because that's not the way it was done in those days. I laughed as I remembered and told my daughter about my promise to myself. I also let her know that she'd one day break any promise she'd make on the subject as well.

The moment passed, but it was one in a series of actions I'm told will continue until she's 21 — embarrassing "mom" moments we cannot control that make our children want to dig holes and jump in.

But spit-wiping her face pales in comparison to other things I've done. For example, I thought she'd die when she caught me dancing in front of her friends.

56

Raising
a
Parent

Now, the problem isn't that I'm not allowed to dance. I was raised on George Clinton and Parliament/Funkadelic. And she and I dance at the house, by ourselves, to the Backstreet Boys, all the time. (See, I've embarrassed her again!)

But she was nearly in tears during a school dance because a little boy asked me to dance, and I accepted. We were the only couple on the floor. And it was so taboo for girls to actually dance with boys that even some grownups stared in amazement, even as they grinned at our rendition of a '90s hustle. I only stopped when I saw her tears becoming real. She couldn't have a good time if I did. So I retreated to my corner to stand watch and warn kids about the slick floor.

Her ultimate continuing embarrassment has been my inability to keep from applauding things. At dinners, at the theater, at ballgames. I'm among the first to show my appreciation for a job well done. At Girl Scout luncheons, I not only clap but give standing ovations to achievers. Every now and then I'll give a whoop and shout, while my daughter bows her head. During soccer matches, I run to the field's edge at every opportunity to cheer the team on

During halftime of one match, I patted backs, yelling, "You go, team! You guys are doing great! You're not far behind! Just hang in there!" I watched her walk away, shaking her head, a look of exasperation mixed with tolerance on her face.

"That's just my mom, guys," she said as she headed for cold water.

Last week, sitting in the semi-darkness at the Tinseltown movie theater, I found encouragement. Before the previews, the theater showed silly slides urging us to clap if we'd ever talked to our food.

I clapped.

57

Raising
a
Parent

It wasn't because I'd had any real conversations. Veggies don't talk back. But I remember coaxing water to boil or asking a carrot to peel evenly. And it seemed appropriate that during "Dr. Doolittle," the new Eddie Murphy movie about a man who talks with animals, I could admit with abandon that I spoke to my veggies.

I wasn't the only one who clapped.

And I bet I wasn't the only one sitting near a little girl whose head was bowed toward the floor, a slight smile and look of exasperation on her face. Because providing "momly embarrassments" is an equal opportunity activity — even dads do it — and I bet I have plenty of company.

What? No "Rudolph!"

My excitement was not shared.

Oh, she tried.

As soon as I suggested an evening of eating hot fudge sundaes and watching "Rudolph the Red-Nosed Reindeer," she tried to be game.

After all, I was excited. This was a show featuring wonderful puppets and classic Christmas songs, a show whose special effects were the 1964 equivalent of "Star Wars." I mean, this show had the Abominable Snowman! But most important, it was a show that I had watched for years as a little girl, one we watched as a family, one I wanted to share with her.

So I was very proud when my daughter clicked us over to CBS and then said, "Oh, boy."

But wait. Her "Oh, boy" sounded like the one reserved for trips to the dentist — well, actually, she likes going to the dentist, so it was more like a trip to the pediatrician. She loves her pediatrician, too, but she hates getting her finger pricked.

What she was doing was trying to make her mom happy, to do something I wanted to do for a change. It was her way of repaying me for the times I rolled around in plastic balls at Discovery Zone (Have you ever FELT those things? They're HARD!) and watched "That Darn Cat" for the 37-hundredth time, or fed her peppermint in church so she wouldn't get bored. This was my turn!

And for about five minutes, she seemed excited I'd chosen a program that had delighted and frightened me nearly every year as a child.

I remember being charmed by "the most famous reindeer of all" and feeling smart

59

Raising a Parent

because I knew that the roly-poly, white-bearded narrator puppet actually looked just like the entertainer who provided his voice, Burl Ives.

The whole program brought back so many wonderful memories of a house with one television instead of two or three, where everyone watched the same show at the same time, where TV dinners were unheard of. You sat at the table and had your dinner, then you watched TV from a favorite perch on the floor, three feet away.

"Rudolph," the longest-running Christmas special there is, was first broadcast in 1964 and recounts how the folks who live in Christmas Town go to the Island of Misfit Toys to get away from the Abominable Snowman, who still scares me.

They eventually get back to Christmas Town, where Rudolph's shiny nose saves Christmas and enables Santa to deliver toys. It was one of my first musicals, with singing and dancing. Some of the songs became classics.

But my daughter eventually grew tired of Christmas Town and wanted instead to head for Nickelodeon and Disneyland, where she spends much of her time now. She was tentative when she asked whether I was enjoying the show.

"Oh, yes. How about you?"

"Well … "

"You wanna watch something else?"

"Only if YOU want to," she answered breathlessly.

So I didn't get scared by the Abominable Snowman, and we didn't get to see Rudolph help save Christmas. But we did have hot fudge sundaes together after having dinner together at a table where we'd talked about school and friends. And

60

Raising
a
Parent

even if we don't share the same tastes in old shows, I hope we're sharing the same tastes in routines and favorite pastimes, like the joy of watching television together.

And she does like some of my stuff: We both can't wait for "How the Grinch Stole Christmas!"

Raising
a
Parent

10 years old

**When preteens need
their privacy**

The privacy question

It was bound to happen sooner or later.

The closed door.

She had just greeted her friend Janessa, who had come over for a slumber party. They grabbed a snack from the kitchen and headed to her room. And I heard the door close.

And I knew that a chapter had closed in our lives, the one whose only characters were mother and daughter, and where there were no secrets.

I didn't have to worry about what they were doing. They were doing what 10-year-olds do: watching television, playing cards and talking about stuff — school, girls they know at school, how silly moms can be.

For the first time in my life, in our lives, I had to knock to see her. Before, I could pass by and receive a quick smile, one that said "Hi, mom," but didn't invite me in.

She's been given her space since she was 6 and I learned that she knew how to play alone. But walking past that closed door made me feel for the first of many times to come as though I was shut out, not needed for the fun. How many times could I actually watch "Rugrats" and enjoy it? (Well, actually, a lot. We saw the movie as much for me as for her.)

When I knocked, there was no giggling, no scurrying to hide the love letters that soon will come from, sigh, boys. There was no hiding of any contraband or anything else that might be untoward. It's not that kind of house. And I, for right now, know. I got an instant invitation to come in. I was asked if I wanted to join in a game of Uno. Reluctantly, I said no. No further entreaties ensued. They went back to their game. And I walked away realizing that I better make some quick memories of this year and this past holiday season.

It might have been the last Thanksgiving when she'd sit without reluctance at the children's table. It might have been the last time she'd want to decorate the Christmas tree with purple balls and little violins that accompany ornaments made from construction paper. It might have been the last Christmas Eve in our pajamas watching movies and waiting for an official visit from Santa.

As I sorted through movies to watch, I kept turning to hers: the Olsen Twins go through some adventure for which they're paid lots of money, or "Flipper" or "That Darn Cat!"

The flood of memories prompted by that closed door was actually pleasant to stroll through, to sort and protect. The door won't always be closed, and some things may remain unchanged. I stopped focusing on the closed door and started thinking about the things I'm still needed for: driving to and from events. The names may change, but my job as James, the chauffeur, will remain the same. It may be a movie date instead of a soccer game, but I'll still be needed.

I bet next Christmas Eve, we'll still sit around in our pajamas watching movies. We can always count on "It's A Wonderful Life" and "That Darn Cat!"

And next New Year's Eve, we'll still be in church. But we probably won't take sketchpads to keep her attention. She sits and listens to our pastor more these days, and asks questions after the sermon.

Sometimes closing some doors means that others are opening.

65

Raising
a
Parent

Making memories

It has become a hauntingly familiar and aching journey.

When my daughter and I recently returned to North Carolina, the place of my past and her future, our visit began on a "street" that is actually a corridor filled with meal carts and the traffic of wheelchair-users pushing themselves around for an afternoon stroll.

Our destinations were two rooms just six doors away from each other, making the visits more convenient, but no less painful. My grandfather and my mother live on the same side of this street; their addresses are in the tony "needs more care" section of the nursing home.

My mother's eyes lit up the moment we entered the room, and she accepted our kisses eagerly without being able to hug us back. Multiple sclerosis has robbed her strength. She laughed heartily and only looked sad when it was time for us to leave.

Down the "street," my grandfather was happy to have visitors, even if he couldn't quite place us. He searched through the names he's collected over 94 years to find mine. Finally, I told him. He grasped it like a cool cup of water, held on and repeated it — "Rochelle! Yeah, Rochelle!" — then lost it and called me by my aunt's name, Lorna Dale.

He rarely leaves the nursing home anymore, so I decided to kidnap him for an adventure.

One of his care workers placed him in the front seat of the rented car. Then we took off — the old man, his granddaughter and his three great-grandchildren — to see his old stomping grounds. He wanted to see the "bend of the river," the Tar River where he grew up and where he fished as a boy. He wanted to see the Sportsman's Club. He once was a member and attended many dances there. We parked at the Pizza Inn to call in an order. I asked him what he wanted most.

"A Pepsi Cola," he said. "I hadn't had one of those in years."

66
Raising
a
Parent

As we sat in the parking lot, three generations of my family had a moment of pure bliss.

When we were done, he wanted more. He wanted to know about former co-workers whose names he hadn't called in years.

"Where's Curt Perkins?" he asked. I remembered Mr. Perkins from my youth but couldn't recall his face and didn't know whether he was alive. But before we started that search, Paw-Paw wanted a hot dog.

So we headed home. As I drove, I tried to figure out how I'd get him in the house, where my grandmother was peeling onions at the kitchen table, as she had for 71 years.

There was a wheelchair on the front porch. I later learned that it was a spare that hadn't been donated to anyone yet. But I know who put it there.

In a burst of unfamiliar strength, I took him out of the car and placed him in the chair. Then we wheeled him up the ramp and into the house.

My grandmother greeted us, kissing him like he'd arrived home from the war. We headed into the kitchen to get the only other thing he wanted as much as a Pepsi.

A hot dog.

Hours later, as his care worker placed him back into his bed, back on the street at the nursing home where he lives six doors from my mother, my grandfather drifted off to sleep.

Tears in his eyes, he said: "This may be the last time I see you."

I told him that wasn't his choice. Somebody else would decide. And in the meantime, he could look forward to another ride. Another Pepsi. And another hot dog.

67

Raising
a
Parent

Booming conclusion ends battle of decibels

I can't recall where I was going, but I remember my car was in the lane next to the one for left turns.

That's where I was when I heard him coming, heard the loud, steady thud of a booming bass. You could hear it for three blocks.

He wasn't working his neck or snapping his fingers or even nodding. He was just sitting, dressed in a baseball cap and a white shirt, surrounded by deafening rap, low, heavy voices like slow jackhammers, a sound you could feel in your heart. He was about 17 years old, clean-cut, looked a little like a young Tom Cruise.

I had been an unwilling audience for so many of these mobile concerts. I could be in the middle of a conversation with my daughter when suddenly we'd realize we couldn't hear each other. So we'd stop talking and look for the show. And sure enough, it would be in a vehicle at least two car lengths away. Yet, we could hear every downbeat, every guitar lick, every word. The Louisville Board of Aldermen — city council in many other places — recently approved a noise ordinance to cut down the decibels. It includes a provision against car stereos that are "plainly audible" 50 feet away.

But I didn't think about calling a police officer as I sat in my car alone. I was thinking I'd had enough. So I fiddled with my radio, searching for just the right tune. Perfect! The Carpenters were singing "Rainy Days and Mondays" — one of my all-time favorite songs — on an oldies station.

I adjusted the bass and treble to levels my radio had never experienced. On a mission, I adjusted the speakers so the sound would rise from the front and the back. Then I turned the volume to a deafening level I hadn't heard in a confined space since those

wild Parliament/Funkadelic parties back in the Upendo Lounge at the University of North Carolina at Chapel Hill.

Then I rolled down the windows.

At first, I didn't look over. I didn't want to pick a fight or to make him angry. I didn't want to compete. I just wanted to make a point. Suddenly, I felt a rising fear. Would he get angry? Would he curse me out, get out of his car?

Then I got angry at myself for feeling fear. People are too afraid of teens, treat them too much like enemies or potential dangers instead of kids looking for adulthood and occasionally getting lost along the way.

What could he do? Throw something at me? He couldn't turn the radio up. There was no volume left.

So I looked over.

He stared straight ahead.

The battle of the bands ensued. It seemed like minutes, but it was only seconds.

Then suddenly, still staring straight ahead, he reached up and turned his radio down, then off.

So I turned my radio down, then off. And we continued to sit.

He stared ahead.

I hoped for a smile, a giggle, an "OK, you win."

I almost said: "Gotcha!"

But I didn't.

He stared straight ahead.

The light changed, the green arrow directing him away from the crazy lady playing

69

Raising
a
Parent

the Carpenters.

He slowly turned and drove away.

I rubbed my ears. And my light changed.

That little standoff was a sweet victory, a win for every person, regardless of age, who thinks mobile concerts without a permit ought to be outlawed. I didn't hear his music come back on, so I don't know if he started booming along again. But I couldn't listen to the radio for the rest of the day, not even the Carpenters.

And I had better get my ears checked.

Raising
a
Parent

Raising
a
Parent

11 years old

**Making memories, living love
and knowing your grandparents**

Hometown flood didn't ruin important things

This Thanksgiving, the turkey and trimmings are not waiting in my hometown of Tarboro, N.C.

They are nowhere near the growing-up house that has defined so much of who I am.

That house is gone, lost in the floods that Hurricane Floyd caused as it stomped around the Carolinas, pushing rivers up and over like a child sloshing through rain puddles.

Instead, we will feast on yams and greens in a townhouse 15 miles away, a place that seems almost sterile without all the treasures from the old house, like the old mahogany table where Thanksgiving dinner had been served since World War II.

As a child I used to look longingly at that table, wanting so much to be a part of the grownup conversation.

Now I wish for the children's table and the innocence of not having to make the decisions, not having to pay the bills, rarely dealing with hatred or prejudice or the tragedy of loss.

As I taste my grandmother's famous (at least in our town) oyster dressing, I'll long just a little for the living-room shelves that were home to all our old pictures: my senior school photo, that dreaded picture from my first prom, the beautiful portrait of my mother in her prime before the ravages of multiple sclerosis took her poised stature.

As we say grace, as we've done hundreds of times over meals prepared with love, I will remember what my grandmother taught me the fall after we lost everything in the waters raised by Hurricane Floyd: We lost nothing.

"I'm too blessed to be distressed," she said.

Returning to my hometown won't be returning to the past anymore. We'll be in a place that has given up the ghost and many of its memories from another time. From now on, it will be a different life, a different millennium, a different town.

Initially, the thought of returning for the holidays saddened me. Walking down streets bearing trailers and the scars of homes that I used to play hide-and-seek behind seemed too much to take.

But I was buoyed not only by the spirits of my grandmother, but also of my daughter, who walked into my bedroom with the 20-year-old doll that my grandmother gave her last year, the doll she named for my mother.

She calls her Marva.

My daughter reminded me that the flood didn't get Marva.

"It's a good thing Moant gave her to me before the flood, huh?" she said.

It was just happenstance that my grandmother passed the doll along when she did. It wasn't a holiday, just one of those unexpected moments between great-grandmother and great-grandchild.

If she hadn't, Marva would be among the mushy remains of memories gone. But instead, she lies in my daughter's room in her blue pajamas (She also has a green velvet dress.), doing what she does best, reminding us that the important things always remain: love, tradition, family.

I remember the last time we transported Marva. It was after my grandmother gave her to my daughter, and my daughter didn't want her packed away, like she wasn't a person. So she carried the heavy doll as far as she could. But, inevitably, she got tired and held her out to me to take. Not so lovingly, I put Marva on the luggage cart, so we could walk the

Raising a Parent

length of the Cincinnati airport in time for our flight to Louisville.

Suddenly, I swerved to avoid a little boy, and Marva sailed off the cart.

And a woman screamed. She thought we'd lost our baby. When my daughter grabbed her by one arm to lift her and put her back, I thought that woman was going to be sick. I rushed to her to explain that Marva was a doll. I held her out for her to touch her.

Relieved, we shared a laugh. I carried Marva the rest of the way.

When we go home, we're taking Marva back, just to let my grandmother see her again and to remind us again that if we have family and our health and love, then we've lost nothing.

The important things always remain.

There's a great man in every family

The sign read: Tarboro, 33 miles.

I've passed it dozens and dozens of times, headed home. It is among the many signs that remind me I've left whatever big city I'm living in and I'm returning to real.

You can tell you're in North Carolina because when you stop at the Bojangles, it's clean, someone wipes the table off before we sit down, and we can hear James Taylor singing on the speakers overhead.

You also know it when you order tea, and it's iced and very sweet.

You can tell when you hear a young man plaintively singing, "One, you're like a dream come true … " — the lyrics from the popular hit "Back at One" — and it's not Brian McKnight, but a country star, singing slower, with a twang.

When we arrived in Tarboro, before heading to places of illness and days' ends, we went to the remains of my growing-up house, the leftovers from Hurricane Floyd's torrents.

There on the ground before me lay about 70 years of bad luck. The 10 big slivers of broken mirror from my grandmother's bedroom represented at least that much, but in all the tiny pieces that lay around it were decades more to come.

Since I knew this would be among my last trips to the old neighborhood, I tried to recapture some of the photographs that lay on the ground, some of the mementos that once meant so much: my niece's little doll, her head turned to the ground as if to hide from the wreckage strewn across the front yard.

Floyd left very little when he marched through, and people are still talking about him. The damage has only begun to resonate for people who lost their homes and cannot build new ones, who lost their health and cannot recapture it, whose spirits are broken and who

77

Raising
a
Parent

don't know their neighbors anymore.

A flood is old news unless it takes so much from you the tears won't stop falling any more than the rain and snow that continue to pelt the tiny towns and beat the spirit out of people who finally, finally give up.

I took those photos of the old house and video of my daughter picking through the wreckage to show them to my Paw-Paw, so he'd have a last look at the home he maintained for his family for nearly 70 years.

I'm proud to be from a small town where drivers still pull over when a funeral procession passes. As our line of cars and trucks meandered through town, headlights on, behind a white hearse, cars pulled over and waited. The tradition is much older than I. Seems it's always been done, except this time it was for my Paw-Paw, and I was trying to steer through tears as we slowly made our way. Our destination was Miss Lovie Rooks' house, which was to serve as a gathering place because my growing-up house had drowned in the floods.

My daughter and I flew in and around ice storms, rented a car and drove on ice-slick roads, all to say goodbye to my beloved Paw-Paw, the grandfather who had been my father since I was 3. He had told me months before that he was ready to go home. Suddenly, months later, he did.

It was a hard trip home, knowing that he wouldn't be there to talk to about my plane ride or to hear me announce that I'd been given two new awards since I last saw him. Both were for being a good role model.

That's what he taught me.

At his funeral, held at the church around the corner because our church drowned last

78

Raising
a
Parent

fall as well, a minister who grew out of a boy I'd known preached that my Paw-Paw was a great man, not because he was the mayor or the richest man in town.

"He could take the simplest things in life and make great from them," the preacher preached. "A great man knows how to invest and make a difference in the lives of people."

My Paw-Paw might have taken the jobs that others wouldn't take, the preacher preached, but because of his investments in his community and in the education of his children, "he changed the destinies of generations."

The preacher was talking about us: my mom, my aunt, my sister and brother, my cousins. We were my Paw-Paw's investments. We brought him interest. We are his legacy.

There is a great man in every family, whether his name be uncle, grandpa, dad or brother. It's not what they do for a living or how much money they make. All that matters is that they invest wisely.

I am my Paw-Paw's investment, and my daughter is mine.

79

Raising
a
Parent

Kids grow up too fast

OK. OK. So I've been caught crying because my daughter is going away to college — in seven years.

And my friends have seen a forlorn look in my eyes because she's going to camp this summer — for a week.

And don't even ask my closest friends, who have shown no surprise at my walking around all mopey and dopey because she's going on an overnight field trip to see some museum and zoo in Columbus and Cincinnati, Ohio. (We've got great museums and a zoo here!)

Yes, I'm exaggerating a little. I made the deliberate choice, with her help, not to go on her next field and camping trips. I'm one of those moms who tends to be involved, and she wants a little more independence.

I want her to see the world, a little bit at a time. I want her to discover new things that scientists don't already know, to send me photos from India, to e-mail me from Sierra Leone. I just want to be there when she does it.

Oh, she's ready. Two weeks before spring break, she said we should spend the holiday in South Africa. I told her we'd have to plan a little more in advance to make that kind of trip. (And she *would* wait until my friend, an American newspaper correspondent there for several years, was just ending her tour of duty.)

My daughter even thinks she's ready to be left home alone. I've thought about it, for maybe 20 minutes or so. Sometimes I pretend to leave, standing in the kitchen, ignoring her orders for room service, just to see her reaction to the possibility that she's alone.

80

Raising a Parent

She just comes and gets her juice herself. She knows how overly protective I am and proud of it.

It's such a shame that we get so mushy when it's time for our children to go somewhere. Whether it's a slumber party a mile away or a weeklong trip hours away, we watch them walk out the door as if it's the last time we'll see them.

When I hear older parents, those whose children are about to make that walk into the world, when they say "I can't wait," I know they don't really mean it.

If they did, then we wouldn't have the Americanism "empty nest" — an expression made up by a tired and retired parent, whose nest wasn't really empty.

There's a bird or two left in it, but many older, lonely birds feel home is empty after the young twerps fly away. They're also saying we don't have to buy for our children anymore, which is good because we don't have any more money. I've always been this way.

Take the first time my daughter was scheduled to ride a bus. She'd never ridden a bus to school, but she was among a group of first-graders who rode a bus from her elementary school to day care across town. I decided to take a break from work, drive over to the school and follow the bus. I laughed when I arrived to find at least five other parents doing the same thing.

No, not one of us was so well-off or bored that we could do that every day. But on that first day, we couldn't resist, watching our watches as we waited for the children to board.

When they trickled out of the school and boarded, one little foot at a time, we raced to our cars and lined up. And we then followed that bus, scared silly little parents that we were.

When the bus got to Lincoln Elementary to pick up more students, we stopped and

81

Raising
a
Parent

waited. When it got back under way, we re-formed our line and the caravan continued to Crescent Hill.

Then we drove back to work, each his or her own way, priding ourselves that we cared so much, wondering whether we were nuts to be so paranoid or slowly reflecting that even if something had happened to the bus, there would have been nothing any of us could have done about it.

In my case, it made me feel better knowing that I could watch that trek that day. And I'll save that memory for all those trips and times in the future when she'll be out on her own, or she'll be hours, or days or weeks away, and I won't be able to watch.

Raising
a
Parent

12 years old

The last birthday that doesn't
have teen in it

12th birthday represents a last chance

My daughter is 12 years old today. It would be any like other birthday except for the way we carve our lives into sections: childhood, teendom, Generation X, Generation Confused, the Pepsi Generation and Baby Doomed, uh, Boomed, and the Golden Years.

So after this final year of childhood, she'll become a person whose age ends in "teen." But what rings greater for me is the farewell to pony rides and Barbie cars, ice cream parties and poofy dresses with yards of taffeta designed solely to itch your legs.

Now, the job becomes simpler yet more complex, as she moves into another phase. It is a phase where I'll get graded by society and grade myself on what I've taught her.

The biggest lesson I hope she'll take into teendom is that she's loved. When I was around her age, birthdays were celebrated as a part of daily living. We were thrilled with birthday cards hiding $5 bills and mouth-watering cakes my grandmother made from scratch. I remember one earlier birthday my grandparents forgot. I moped around, dragging my feet, my eyes downcast until my grandfather finally asked "What's the matter with you?"

"It's my birthday," I told him. "And everybody forgot."

The look in his eyes made up for every bad thought I'd had that morning. My Paw-Paw leaned forward in the La-Z-Boy recliner that he lived in on the weekends, reached into his front pocket, the change pocket, the one we used to stare at on Friday evenings because we'd just die for a nickel to run around the corner to the store where you could buy 25 cookies for that single coin.

He reached in and handed me a dime. It was a new one, pretty and full of a bigger story than 10 pennies can tell.

I kept that dime for a long time — at least two days — before heading around the

corner to the store. But I kept that memory for a long, long time. That dime healed what might have been a bigger wound and reminded me that I was loved.

Teendom requires simpler, but more important gifts. This will be my last year to help her review the materials I've given her for life. Next year, when she actually becomes a teen, it will be too late.

Oh, I can remind her. I can try to be a role model for lessons learned. But more often than not, I won't be there for the tests. She'll be hanging out with friends. She'll be riding in cars with boys.

As I mourn with strangers in Grosse Pointe Woods whose teenage children's lives ended last week in a night shattered by a loud crash and a louder heartbreak, I know that, beginning in a few years, there but for the grace of God go I.

I know my daughter will, on some nights, face situations I can't talk her through, and I won't know until later whether she followed the rules.

She'll have to decide not to drink or smoke or be tempted by a sweet smile and a great come-on. She'll have to decide whether to call home when the choice is between waking me or climbing in with a drunk driver. (She should know I don't sleep when she's out.)

For this birthday, besides useless but fun gifts, I plan to give her a dime. It won't pay for a phone call anymore. But I hope it will represent for her what my Paw-Paw's dime meant to me — a lifetime of love and a reminder of the things that cannot be bought, the things that, as our children grow older, they must remember without us.

I hope it will help her remember the greatest two lessons: Tomorrow isn't promised, but it can be given away, quickly, with one bad choice. And no mistake is too great to take to a parent.

Raising
a
Parent

For everything else, there's a mom's love

Canceling a trip to New Orleans to hang out at the Essence Music Festival: $296.

That was the cost of four unused tickets to hear the Isley Brothers and India.Arie, Luther Vandross and Frankie Beverly and Maze.

It would have been the first concert I'd attended since Jill Scott and Sting sang at the Palace last year.

It would have been the first time I'd seen one of my best friends, Janet, since she came for Thanksgiving dinner last November. We only get to see each other two or three times a year, which is about 50 times less than I'd like, but a blessing whenever it happens.

It would have been my first time in New Orleans in more than a decade, having missed every Mardi Gras I'd ever hoped to make because of work or school commitments.

And it would have been my first trip with a new Detroit friend who has made living here a greater joy.

Visiting Target to find just the right standing fan for a lakeside cabin with 12 girls in it: $94.19.

The fan only cost $39.99. But I've never shopped at Target without buying more than I went in for.

I can walk into Target for a $2.99 toothbrush but still wind up buying a shirt, a book, some snacks and at least one of something that's on sale. On this trip, my bill included $2.69 for a National Enquirer (yes, I sometimes read it, and yes, I paid $2 more than I should have), insect repellant, two bags of smoothie mix (you blend it with ice and water, and, as the new It drink, it's supposed to replace fresh fruit), two pillows and, of course, that 4-foot fan, which was all I had wanted in the first place.

Driving to northern Michigan to take that fan because the heat spell that hit the country last week didn't skip Grand Traverse Bay and its surrounding communities:

Driving to northern Michigan because I got a phone call, and a small voice on the other end said, "I don't want to stay at camp. It's hot and I can't sleep, and I'm so tired. Can I please come home?"

Driving to northern Michigan and being greeted in the woods by a hot, tired 12-year-old who hugged me so tight that I gasped, and who, for the first time, didn't let go first:

Priceless.

And it didn't even matter that the temperature had already dropped nearly 20 degrees, because she was as glad to see me as the fan.

Sometimes when I think that I'm missing out on my life because my life became my daughter's life from the moment she arrived, I have only to remember that the life I chose with her is the only one I really want.

It is her smile that brightens my day. It is her 'A' on a test that I celebrate as much any column I write.

It is her art that I buy special frames for and hang on the walls of our home right along with Romare Bearden and Ellis Wilson.

And when I think of 3-year-old Adonnis and 10-month-old Acacia Maynor, whose mother left them in a hot car in Southfield, where they slowly and painfully died, and little Amari Ware, who died after a bullet burned its way into its stomach, when I think of those children, I cry.

I cry for those parents who are parents too young and too soon and who don't understand the magnitude of the lives in their hands.

I cry for neighbors and relatives who watch those too-soon, failing parents but do nothing.

I cry for myself as I pledge to be a better parent, which makes it so simple to cancel a concert for the joy of driving five hours to take a fan to camp.

In fact, it was the easiest decision in the world.

Raising
a
Parent

13 years old

Terrible teens:
Becoming someone new and
changing their names

Some kids just want to be different

It happens with kids. They have a bad day and want to go into the witness protection program. They have a school dance coming up and would rather fake a stomachache than dance in front of kids of the opposite sex. And sometimes, they just want to be different.

They wake up and dye their hair or ask for a tattoo or beg to pierce some place that hurts.

Thank goodness my daughter hasn't asked for a tattoo, and she's too young to get into the color of the week thing. But she did bring up something last week that she wants to change: her name. It's not that she hates the name I gave her. It has suited her and served her well for a while.

But her preparations for high school have meant more than figuring out which designer's clothes will become her signature style. It means more than deciding whether she's an actress first or singer first, or veterinarian instead of an artist. It means taking on a moniker that is hip, exciting and something I wouldn't have chosen. That's a requirement. If I like it, it doesn't work.

In her case, she wants to be Nikki. Not Nicole. Not Nicoletta. Just Nikki.

I held out hope that at some time, I'd mentioned Nikki Giovanni, the Knoxville, Tenn., native who edited the literary magazine at Fisk University, organized Cincinnati's Black Arts Festival and offered reflections on African-American identity that were unique in the '60s and '70s. Her poetry sustained me in college, and her "Ego Tripping" remains my favorite poem. It reads, in part:

92

Raising
a
Parent

I was born in the congo
I walked to the fertile crescent and built
the sphinx
I designed a pyramid so tough that a star
that only glows every one hundred years falls
into the center giving divine perfect light
I am bad

I sat on the throne
drinking nectar with allah
I got hot and sent an ice age to europe
to cool my thirst
My oldest daughter is nefertiti
the tears from my birth pains created the nile
I am a beautiful woman.

I gazed on the forest and burned
out the sahara desert
with a packet of goat's meat
and a change of clothes
I crossed it in two hours
I am a gazelle so swift
so swift you can't catch me

For a birthday present when he was three
I gave my son hannibal an elephant
He gave me rome for mother's day
My strength flows ever on ...

93

Raising
a
Parent

But there was nothing profound or literary about my daughter's choice of Nikki. She just liked the sound of it. So I treated this flight of fancy like any other. I put the onus on her and explained that she'd have to earn $250 to change her name. She, of course, was apoplectic!

"Why!?" she queried in the plaintive wail of teenage angst.

I explained: She'd need $125 for legal fees, $90 for a new passport and $10 for the doctor's visit.

"What doctor's visit?" she asked.

"The one where you get all your school shots over again under your new name." I told her. "Your co-pay is $10."

I haven't heard anything about the name change since.

And I didn't even get the chance to tell her that Nikki Giovanni's real name was Yolanda Cornelia.

Raising
a
Parent

Raising
a
Parent

14 years old

**Missing clothes and
other surprises**

Life's never dull with a teen around

You know you're the parent of a teenager when:

• You can't find your clothes, particularly the ones you don't wear outside (like baggy pants, the shirt with spots from the last paint job and your favorite Joe Boxer pajama bottoms).

• Entire juice cartons disappear from the refrigerator like socks from the dryer.

• There is always a last-minute math test, even one that was announced last month.

• Boys call and ask for your only child, and you want their name, age and Social Security number before handing over the phone.

But you really know you're the parent of a teenager when you begin to exchange the stories with other parents. You know the ones. Sure, all parents brag:

"My child made an 'A' on that test."

"Well, my child could teach that test!"

But the stories I'm talking about are the tales of "You won't believe what they did this time!"

I've had my share of stories. My daughter has been so grounded at times that I've had to think of a new word for it. And I thought I had the story of the week when I arrived home last week to find the entire house filled with smoke. Our dog, Lucy, was panting at the garage door, and my daughter was nowhere to be seen. Smoke had drifted into every room. I couldn't shake the image in my head of her lying somewhere, suffering from smoke inhalation. I was scared to death until I saw a kitchen window open, and I could hear my kid walking around upstairs.

"What's going on? Are you all right? What happened?"

98

Raising
a
Parent

She calmly descended and walked casually to the sink.

"What do you mean?" she asked innocently through the haze. "Is something wrong?"

For a minute I saw Derrick Boone, a guy a year ahead of me in college who loved showing freshmen the ropes. He taught me that the best initial line of defense for any misdemeanor was "Deny. Deny. Deny."

I looked at my daughter as if she were from another planet. "Do you not see all this smoke? What were you doing?"

"I just cooked some bacon," she said. "You want some?"

When I recounted the story to my friend Shelley, she was ready. But her story wasn't about her own kids. It was about her friend Diane's son, an introvert who'd rather read a book than attend a basketball game. To improve his social life, his mom made him go to a basketball game, figuring he would meet people, maybe talk to somebody. So he went, sat at the nosebleed level and read a book.

A reporter spotted him in the rowdy crowd and asked why he was there. His reply?

"Because my mom made me. She said if I didn't come here, I had to go to some old lady's birthday party."

The following Sunday morning, Diane's phone rang off the hook with friends asking whether she'd seen the newspaper. She asked her son about the game, asked whether he'd met any new friends, whether he talked to anybody.

Nope, he said.

"You sure?" she asked.

He was sure. So she showed him the paper, pointing to his quote.

Unimpressed, he told her that adults don't count.

It'll take me a while to top that one.

99

Raising
a
Parent

15 years old

The Final Frontier

A mother-daughter report card

In the weeks before I became a mom, my Aunt Nell said something to me that may be the most important thing any parent can remember: Parenting is unrelenting.

It is not a negative statement.

It is a realistic assessment of what it means to be responsible for a person for the rest of life. Your life. Not theirs. Every Mother's Day, I send a thank-you heavenward to my grandmother for what I now know was eternal patience. All those things she taught me that I thought were just to ruin my life make so much sense now, and I can only hope she knows I finally get it.

She gave me a moral core that governs how I raise my daughter. Every Mother's Day, I say a silent prayer for my mother, who was lucky to have a mother who could step in and assume her role while she battled her own decades-long illness.

And every Mother's Day, I take time to assess how I'm doing. I create a report card based on my daughter's achievements, challenges and complaints, and I list her grades and mine:

• On letting my daughter, who is 15, make decisions regarding her life: My daughter gives me a C- because she thinks that everyone else's mom gives their children more freedom than I give her. I would score myself at B because, as I've explained to her, she can make any decisions in her life that have nothing to do with money. And since malls and teen clubs and R-rated movies and trips to Cancun all cost money, I can regulate those things even without considering the moral and intrinsic value of each.

• On letting my daughter wear skimpy clothes: My daughter would grade me a D, and I would grade myself a B. It has become a daily debate, this discussion about whether clothes appropriate for a Ciara video are appropriate for school. I try to recall what it was like in

102

Raising
a
Parent

high school, when I felt that my grandparents were fashion snobs who had no idea what cool was. But as much as I remember my complaints, I also remember wearing a yellow popcorn bodysuit with hip-hugger jeans. So they must have relented occasionally, as do I.

• On letting my daughter date: I wasn't allowed to date until I was 18, and by then I'd decided I'd rather wait until college. Since my daughter knows the sacrifice I'm making in changing a family tradition and letting her date at 16, we both grade me a B.

• On letting my daughter have unfettered access to the Internet: She would give me an F, and I would grade myself an A. Few chat rooms. No e-mails to strangers. No porn sites, dating sites or sites where I think pedophiles might hang out. She says she may as well not use the computer. I tell her using it just for homework isn't a bad idea. We'll compromise eventually, but I explain to her that it's like driving. She's not the problem. The other drivers are.

• On regulating my daughter's television-watching: She rates me a C. I think I've earned an A. She gets to watch videos in the afternoons and "Fear Factor" when homework is done. (Since neither expands her mind, I should earn an A-plus.)

Now, I know that some of you are saying: Why let your daughter grade you?

Because we can learn from our children.

It can be something as simple as not using the phrase "hook up" because it means "to have sex." It can be as complex as what dreams mean. I'm just glad to be a parent who still has conversations with her teen.

So that's a C-, a D, a B, an F and a C on her card, and three Bs and two As on mine. And though I take her card seriously, mine will keep her out of trouble, get her into college and make sure the person I turn loose on society will be welcomed instead of avoided.

103

Raising
a
Parent

16 years old

First dances, the rules of dress
and lasting boyfriends

First lesson is good sense

It is time to shop for back-to-school items, and unfortunately, with each passing year, the trip requires more shopping in the mall of ideals and common sense than in malls where Target and Marshall Field's rule.

These days, particularly for the parents of teenagers, helping our kids find what they need for school means helping them look for more challenging items than a graphing calculator and three-ring binders.

We must help them look for their moral centers, something lacking in many students whose parents have thrown up their hands and given up on discipline, challenge and expectations, and given in to whining, peer pressure and keeping up with the Diddies.

Our kids learn plenty from rap and hip-hop music about protecting their "goodies" and visits to the "candy shop." They learn from each other that sex is no longer a big deal, that hooking up means just that — the kind of casual sex that used to exist only in movies that teenagers couldn't see. At least 28% of 15-year-olds in America are having sex, according to a recent poll conducted by NBC and People magazine. Twenty-nine percent are engaging in oral sex, which some kids don't think is sex at all.

As someone who wasn't allowed to date until I was 18 — "back in the Dark Ages," as my daughter describes those times — I find it distressing to see a growing blatant sexuality that didn't start with Britney Spears and won't end with Ciara.

More and more, girls are dressing like prostitutes, while boys wear twice the clothes they used to. The attire is not only expected — and accepted at most high schools — but is required to fit in. Teens are learning that being too smart means you're not down, and acting ignorant might get you a record deal, except there are only a couple of hundred such deals each year for

106

Raising
a
Parent

the couple of million kids who want them.

There is a growing decline among teens in self-respect, morality and innocence. I don't need a study to tell me. I see how they dress and their public makeout sessions. I hear from the high school students that I mentor about the trysts in vacant classrooms and disappearances from school for quick hookups while parents are at work.

While we're packing backpacks this month to send our teens into workplaces where work is no longer Job One and being popular and having fun get more attention, we need to send them with more than books and pencils. We need to send them with reminders that there's still a place for discipline and ambition, for achievement and morality. We need to help them make room for self-respect and the ability to say no. We need to remind them that you don't have to be down, or hip, if being down really does take you down.

Sometimes, it's OK to be the nerd, to be the one who gets teased for being right, for being honest, for having a moral center.

Raising
a
Parent

Stand back; let her dance

As I watched her run around setting out her clothes and choosing just the right purse and shoes from my closet, I kept wondering: Where has time gone? As she primped in front of a mirror doing her own hair, I kept wondering what my role was. I had nothing to do.

And as my daughter emerged from her room in a red satin gown, wearing my black evening sandals and carrying my black silk purse made like a Chinese take-out box, I kept seeing my 2-year-old about to go to her first homecoming dance.

I know she's 16.

And it's not that I haven't been there for every minute of the roller coaster ride that is raising a child — the first field trip, first lunch box, first Crayon set, first paint set, first bra, all on the road from pigtails to curls.

It's not that I wasn't listening as her music moved from Barney ("I love you. You love me.") to the Backstreet Boys to Usher to Pretty Ricky. I've been there for all of it. But it sometimes seemed like it was happening to someone else. And as I watched my beautiful girl twirl in a satin gown, I kept looking for that 2-year-old who used to sit on my lap and eat Popsicles.

Instead, a woman twirled, her back perfectly straight, her hair perfectly coiffed. She said, "Well, Mom, how do I look?"

And for just a moment, what I saw was my 2-year-old twirl in her first Sunday dress, one that she chose herself, her 2-year-old eyes glowing with pride at her choice.

What I saw was a 10-year-old twirl around in her first cheerleader uniform, an amazing fifth-grader who, even as she yelled her loudest at the game, would still sneak a peek at the bleachers to make sure I was there. What I saw was an 11-year-old twirl around in a blue taffeta miniature cocktail dress as I dragged her to the first of many formal dinners and speeches where she'd sit and endure me talking about how proud I was of her.

When your child turns 16, it is time to let go of that bicycle of life and let her begin to pedal on her own, watch her use the lessons you've taught her. That's why I said, "Oh, that's nice" when she told me that instead of going to the dance with the date she'd chosen, she was going with a group of girlfriends.

And that's why, when the dance was over, and she drove to a nearby restaurant for the after-set, I said, "Have fun."

And that's why, when the evening was over, I could only say, "You're welcome, baby" when she threw her arms around my neck and said, "Thanks, Mom!" — the same way she did when she got her first tricycle and when she got her first puppy and when she got a new video to watch.

As she headed off to bed, I sat and remembered the scene from earlier in the evening — a young woman twirling in red satin. But this time, I could see glimpses of a 2-year-old modeling her first dress, her eyes bright with pride and the possibilities to come.

She's still there, after all.

109

Raising
a
Parent

Your First Car.

Everybody Wants...

Everybody Gets...

17 years old

**The Final Chapter:
First cars and prom nights**

The car

I tried to make it a big deal, like a first dance or first date. Unfortunately, there was nothing monumental about buying my daughter her first car. You live in Detroit. You need a vehicle.

But the rite of passage was special in this: Not once while buying six other cars did I ever think about the person who assembled the chassis or attached the steering wheel or polished the hood. I never thought about whether I lived near the plant. I'd never seen a car come off a line before. My hometown newspapers didn't carry headlines about auto plants or stories about new models before you could buy them.

Ten years ago, if someone had said "concept car" to me, I would have thought it was a name, like Element. But this is Motown, which stood for cars before it stood for music, so the rite of passage — buying your child her first car — is an experience in being a Detroiter, in loyalty and quality as much as insurance and tires.

She rejected a new car. She is now a true Detroiter, and all the cars she likes are older models. She gained needed ammunition from my insurance agent. What it costs to insure a 17-year-old is nothing short of immoral.

Our journey to first car also taught me how much of a Detroiter my daughter has become. She not only can name almost any car on the road, she can tell the difference in the same car from one year to the next. Me? I think all sedans look like Tauruses and all SUVs look like Explorers.

She can tell you which cars come with spoilers. I can't tell you what a spoiler is. She can tell you when a car was discontinued. Cars for me are pricier alternatives to trains.

When I lived in Washington, D.C., I took the Metro. In New York, I take the subway.

Raising
a
Parent

In Dallas, I learned to hate roads.

Detroit is Dallas 20 years ago.

Our search began with my online comparisons of different models, their gas mileage and Edmunds values. She perused dozens of used-auto magazines she found outside restaurants and Blockbuster. While I extolled the virtues of Consumer Reports rankings, she wondered whether the cars had rims. And a spoiler apparently is necessary or the car won't start.

While I talked economy, she expressed frantic doubt that we'd find her car before the first day of school. With each dealer visit, I'd ask about mileage and the trunk space. She wanted to know what kind of stereo it had. At every stop, I called my insurance agent. She called her friends.

Finally, we found her car, a 2000 black Mercury Cougar with a spoiler, at the Motor City Auto Auction in Fraser. It was sitting on the lot with her name on it. No, not literally. But the way she screamed that it was hers, I thought it must be. It has gray leather seats, new wheels and a good engine. It has a stereo and CD player, and it takes about $28 bucks to fill it up.

But that's OK. She drives two weeks on a tank of gas, since she rarely drives more than 10 miles from our house, and she just informed me that when it begins to snow, she's taking the bus.

Raising
a
Parent

The prom

As I write this, I'm getting ready for my last prom.

We found the gown six weeks ago, a coral empress with a shirred bodice and an Egyptian-style collar. We called 17 limo companies to find a silver one. We found the right date — the tall, handsome son of family friends.

Now, it's all over except for the photos. Then, that will be it for me. The "we" becomes "she," and my daughter will embark on one of her last senior experiences, on a Tuesday, no less. Her school plans events for nearly every night of graduation week, and Tuesday prom is tradition.

Tradition.

That's what prom has always meant. So I will sit by the clock and reflect on something as time-honored as a softball game on a hot evening or eating candy apples while walking a state fair midway.

This is how pervasive prom is. We don't ask whether someone went; we ask them to relive it. My friend LaTanya was a serial prom date who attended nine dances. But her own prom was a disaster. She and her boyfriend had a fight, and she told him to find another date.

"And he did," she said with raucous laughter.

My friend Amanie Mokdad, 36, a married mother of three from Canton, is Lebanese and blessed not to have been the oldest girl.

"My sister who's four years older had to go with my brother, which was just traumatizing for her."

Amanie could have gone with a date to her prom but chose to watch a Detroit

Raising
a
Parent

Pistons game with her dad instead. By the time her youngest sister's prom came, her parents had evolved.

"We went from my sister who couldn't even have a boyfriend to the youngest who was going through boyfriends every three weeks. I think they just got tired of us. They got to: 'Whatever! You want a boyfriend, go get one.'"

My grandparents were staunch Christians who grew up before World War II. I wasn't allowed to date until I was 18, four months before prom. So I couldn't understand why my grandmother was excitedly trying to find the right dress.

"You're kidding, right?" I asked. "I couldn't date, remember? Who's going to take me?"

Never ask that question of a Southern grandmother who never met a problem she couldn't solve. She set me up with a friend's son, a quiet, studious boy who, like me, spent more time in books than on dates.

My humiliation continued when she picked out my dress, a floral gown with long sleeves, very long sleeves, almost Victorian sleeves, over a girdle that wouldn't come off even if three boys tried.

We went to the prom and sat on the bleachers for as long as we thought necessary to make my grandma happy. Then I went out to dinner.

Maybe prom memories are more important than the dances. If you think we have nothing in common, ask a stranger about prom. Between the laughter, we can learn how similar we truly are.

Raising
a
Parent

The time … where did it go?

I have to stop counting milestones. We all expect them. Entire books have been written to honor them, learn about them, point out what is normal about them.

The problem is: When we spend too much time counting them, we sometimes forget to live them.

Take children, for instance. We mark their first words, first steps, first time reading, first art project, first chapter book, first time swinging by themselves, first swim, first gold medal, blue ribbon, speech, essay, standardized test, graduation from elementary school, middle school and high school. As soon as one milestone passes, we look forward to the next one.

My daughter attended her first and last prom Tuesday night. She looked like a princess, like a too-gorgeous-to-be-real character from a Walt Disney movie whose picture-perfect Cinderella date became a series of photographs, a coral gown lying in a heap and memories we don't have time to relish because graduation is today.

Wait! Stop. Don't move.

I want to wallow in the moment when she walked out of the front door on her friend's arm, looking as glamorous as any movie star on a red carpet. I want to rewind her graceful entry into a silver stretch limo. I want to watch it pull away again, as I stand with a tear in my eye, slightly choking on the thought stuck in my throat that I'm really going to have to give her up soon, give her to the world and her own decisions and her own path.

The dancing and strolling supper and paparazzi moments over, she moved ahead without blinking to the next milestones, the next decisions: What to wear under the stiff,

sheer, white graduation gown; what to wear to the all-night party that will follow tonight, and what to do with possibly her last summer at home.

She's talking about college …

Wait, hold on, don't go so fast.

I'm remembering when she was 5 and had two hamsters, Abra and Cadabra. She's talking dorm room, and I'm remembering her first day at school when she traded my hand for her kindergarten teacher's.

I was supposed to be on Mackinac Island this week for the Detroit Regional Chamber's annual policy conference, joining everybody who is somebody to try to figure out ways to save the state. Regionalism is all the buzz. Labor leaders urge togetherness. Great change seems within reach. But I can't be bothered with state affairs, not in the days leading up to graduation. I don't want to talk about the budget crisis or charter schools.

No, I'm holding a photo of my daughter and her cheerleading squad at the regional competition last spring, a frame full of bright eyes and huge smiles. I see America in their faces. I see hope and opportunity and mothers and senators and, possibly, the third female president of the United States. I look into my daughter's face, and realize I can't help save the state this week. I must stop and focus on this moment, this milestone, this child.

I have a higher mission on this, my daughter's high school graduation day:

Save the cheerleader. Save the world.

Raising
a
Parent

Far left: Rochelle and Therese Riley when Therese was 2.

Left: Mother and daughter at high school graduation 16 years later.

Afterword

Our agreement was that when my daughter turned 17, I would stop sharing her every move with tens of thousands of strangers. My daughter has graduated high school. She is navigating the world from a different perch. Her stories are hers to tell now. The greatest lesson my daughter taught me is that when children become grown-ups, you no longer control them. Like birds pushed out of nests to fly, you must watch while they choose their own paths, make their own memories, travel their own journeys. She's traveling her own journey … and I'm still watching … still loving … still learning.

Index of Book Illustrations

119

*Raising
a
Parent*

Calling All Parents!

Would you like to share your stories about growing up with your child?

Rochelle is seeking parent essays to be featured in her 2011 book "Raising A Parent: Lessons Our Children Have Taught Us." It's an opportunity for you to share wonderful, funny or even heartbreaking moments from your lives with your children.

Please send your 500- to 700-word essays to:

RAISING A PARENT
Church Street Media
P.O. Box 7044
Ann Arbor, Michigan, 48107

or e-mail to: rochelle@raisingaparent.com

The deadline is August 1, 2010.

Raising
a
Parent